Canadian Payroll for Ontario

A Complete Guide for Small Business

R obi n L ao

Tellwell Talent
www.tellwell.ca

ISBN
978-0-2288-0908-1 (Hardcover)
978-0-2288-0907-4 (Paperback)
978-0-2288-0909-8 (eBook)

Table of Contents

PART 1
Getting Started: Payroll Set Up

PART 2
Employment Standard Acts

PART 3
Employee Set Up

PART 4
Payroll Processing

PART 8
Appendices

F o r e w o r d

This book is specifically written for Canadian small businesses. It is a one-stop reference tool to demystify Canadian payroll. This book introduces the basic concepts of payroll, accurate and efficient payroll processing, provincial employment standards and CRA tax regulations.

Topics include the following:

- tax information for Ontario;
- federal and Ontario employment standards;
- step-by-step examples of payroll processing using a free payroll tax calculator; and
- links to important websites.

After reading this book, you should be able to:

- process a payroll, calculate pay, remit taxes and prepare year-end T4s;
- understand CRA regulations and requirements;
- understand federal and provincial employment standards relating to employees;
- calculate payroll taxes, CPP and EI using a free online pay calculator; and
- learn best practices for payroll processing.

Benefits include:

- understanding basic concepts of payroll processing;
- learning federal and Ontario employment standards;
- saving time and effort in processing payroll; and
- saving money by doing payroll yourself.

Who should read this book?

- small business owners with employees;
- anyone interested in learning about Canadian payroll;
- students in accounting or human resources who need basic payroll knowledge;
- human resources and payroll professionals who need a basic reference book on Canadian payroll;
- employees who want to learn how payroll is done; and
- payroll/accounting course instructors who might want to use this book to teach payroll.

Errors and omissions excepted (E&OE). The author will not be held responsible if an error has been committed in the publication of this book, as information may have changed by the time of use.

For feedback, corrections and suggestions, please email: feedback@hrclub.ca

Government websites, sample forms, guides and future updates discussed in this book will be available at www.hrclub.ca/book

Introduction

I have hired my first employee. What do I need to know to set up payroll to satisfy the government and my employees and ensure my business needs are met? These are questions that many first-time employers ask.

As an Ontario employer, you are responsible for paying your employee in a timely manner while complying with Ontario employment standards. You must deduct federal and provincial income taxes, Canada Pension Plan (CPP) contributions and Employment Insurance (EI) premiums prior to paying your employees. In some cases, overtime, vacation and holiday pay are paid when the employee is eligible to receive them. Taxes, CPP and EI deductions from the employee plus the company- matching CPP and EI must be sent to the Canada Revenue Agency (CRA) according to a remittance schedule.

In the following pages, you will be shown all the basics of Canadian payroll and everything a small business person needs to comply with. You will learn how to properly remit employee deductions and employer contributions to the CRA. You will also learn how to process employee T4s and submit copies to the CRA.

The idea is to make it easy for you to understand payroll concepts to do your own payroll, either with software or online payroll calculators, saving you the cost of outsourcing payroll processing.

This book covers:

- Employment Insurance, Canada Pension Plan, TD1 and T4 forms;
- payable work hours, overtime, vacation, holiday and other types of pays;
- federal and provincial taxes, employer and employee CPP contributions and EI premiums;
- pay stubs, CRA remittances, year-end T4s and other reporting requirements; and
- a step-by-step example of how to process a payroll.

> This book concentrates on the most important and relevant knowledge required by small businesses. Large company related topics such as unions, company shares, pensions, etc. will not be covered.

About the Author

Robin Lao is the founder of HR Club Inc. He earned his bachelor's and master's degrees in Computer Science at the University of Wisconsin.

Robin has served as an MIS Manager for Canadian Tire Corporation, responsible for the development and support of its in-house HR and payroll system.

Robin co-founded the CHRSP (Canadian Human Resource System Professionals) in 1986. He served as its first president and director for three years.

In 2001, HRIS Consultants Ltd. developed a payroll software for small businesses named "WinTax." In 2012, a free online payroll calculator version was developed. This calculator is still being used by thousands of users.

The first-hand experience gained by Robin over 35 years in HR and payroll, particularly with the development and support of the WinTax payroll software, is the basis for the contents of this book.

Researcher/Editor — Linda Trabulsi

Worked as an Executive Assistant and has several years working as a payroll administrator.

Contributor — Joyce Diaz, CHRP, CPM

Member of the Canadian Payroll Association and Human Resource Professional Association with many years of experience as an HR and payroll manager.

PART 1

Getting Started: Payroll Set Up

This section explains how to set up business accounts, payroll accounts and government services. It also covers information on how to set up payroll processing for the entire employment cycle.

The payroll process requires that all rules and regulations of the Ontario employment standards be followed. Company benefits and policies can be different as long as they meet the minimum requirements of the employment standards.

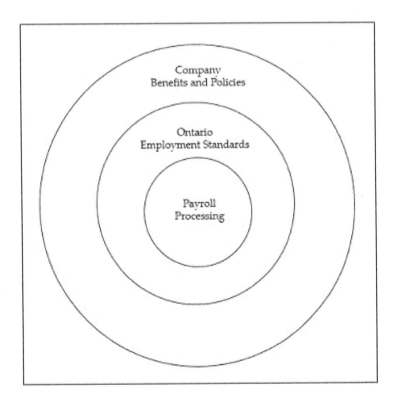

Chapter 1

Setting Up Payroll Accounts

1.1   Business Accounts

A business number (BN) is a unique number that allows the Canada Revenue Agency (CRA) to identify a business (or other organization, such as a charity) for tax matters related to businesses in Canada. It is also used by the federal, provincial and municipal governments to identify the business. Each business requires one business number for its legal entity. A legal entity is defined as a sole proprietorship, partnership, corporation, trust or other organization.

The BN has 15 characters: nine unique numbers to identify the business, plus two letters and four more numbers to identify the program and each account.

The four major program accounts are identified by the following:

- RT Goods and services tax/harmonized sales tax (GST/HST)
- RP Payroll
- RM Import-Export
- RC Corporation income tax

These are examples of registered accounts:

- Business Number (BN) 12345 6789
- GST/HST program account 12345 6789 RT 0001
- Payroll program account 1 12345 6789 RP 0001
- Payroll program account 2 12345 6789 RP 0002
- Import/Export program account 12345 6789 RM 0001
- Corporation income tax 12345 6789 RC 0001

1.2   Payroll Program Account Number

Employers must register for a payroll program account before the first remittance due date. A payroll program account is an account number assigned to either an employer, a trustee or a payer of other amounts related to employment to identify them when dealing with the CRA.

This 15-character payroll program account number contains the following:

- the nine-digit BN;
- two letters for the type of account (for payroll program the letters are "RP"); and
- four numbers for the specific account reference.

Depending on the type of business you have, you may need to register other types of program accounts. The nine-digit registration number will not change, but other letters will be added to the BN.

If you are a new remitter, your first remittance due date is the 15th day of the month following the month in which you began withholding deductions from your employee's pay.

Chapter 2

Registering for Government Services

2.1 Record of Employment (ROE WEB)

Steps to register for Record of Employment on the ROE Web:

1. Sign-in to ROE Web through a Sign-In Partner or a GCKey. If you need a GCKey, click the 'Continue to GCKey' button. Click 'Sign Up' button on the 'Welcome to GCKey' screen to create your unique GCKey, which is the Government of Canada's log-in password.

2. Create your professional profile—this includes name and contact information. A user reference number will be emailed to you.

3. Create the profile of the organization. Validate the organization by providing the organization's Canada Revenue Agency (CRA) business number.

4. Authenticate your identity online through CRA. Enter your authorization code. If you have not already registered for the CRA My Account, the registration process could take five to ten business days, after which time you will be required to sign back in to ROE Web to finalize the authentication process. Identity validation can also be done in person.

5. Enter your authorization code—this code confirms your authority to act as Primary Officer on behalf of the organization.

6. Read and accept the agreement.

7. Start issuing electronic ROEs.

2.2   Employer Health Tax (EHT)

Employer Health Tax (EHT) is a payroll tax on wages paid to employees and former employees.

You need to register with the province if you are an employer and you are:

- not eligible for the tax exemption;
- eligible for the tax exemption and your Ontario payroll exceeds your allowable exemption amount; or
- an associated employer.

For more information regarding EHT exemption, refer to Chapter 11.6.

2.3   Workplace Safety & Insurance Board (WSIB)

Most businesses in Ontario that employ workers (including family members and sub-contractors) must register with the WSIB within ten days of hiring their first full- or part-time employee. The WSIB collects assessments from most employers in Ontario, pooling them in a collective liability fund and then distributing benefits to employees who are injured from occupational accidents.

Chapter 3

Employer Payroll Setup

3.1 Determining Payroll Frequency

You must decide whether your employees will be salaried or paid hourly. The most common pay frequency for salaried employees is bi-weekly, or every two weeks, on the last day of the two-week period. Hourly employees are usually paid weekly or bi-weekly. As the hours worked are never the same on a daily basis, payroll processing would occur two or three days after the end of the pay period.

3.2 Preparing a Payroll Schedule

The pay date or cheque date is very important when dealing with the CRA. This date, not to be confused with the pay period end date, is used to determine the CRA tax year and which pays are included in the T4 and T4 summary for the taxation year.

Depending on your established payday, every several years, a weekly pay schedule will have 53 pays instead of the regular 52 pays. A bi-weekly schedule will have 27 pays instead of the regular 26 pays.

For example, if a payday falls on the first Friday of January, there will be 53 pays for weekly and 27 pays for bi-weekly payrolls in the years 2021 and 2027.

The gross pay of a pay period multiplied by the pay frequency (the number of times employees are paid) is the estimated annual income. This estimated annual income is used by the CRA to determine the employee's tax bracket for calculating federal and provincial taxes.

If you keep the 26 bi-weekly pay frequency in a 27 pay tax year:

- a pay of $2,000 on a 26 pay frequency will result in an estimated annual income of $52,000. A pay of $2,000 on a 27 pay frequency will result in an estimated annual income of $54,000, an increase of $2,000 for the tax year;
- taxes deducted are not sufficient because the tax calculation did not account for the additional $2,000 extra earned for the year; and
- when filing a T4 slip for the taxation year, the employee will owe taxes.

However, if the pay frequency is changed from a 26 to 27 pay frequency in a 27 tax year:

- a bi-weekly pay of $2,000 will result in an estimated annual income of $54,000, an increase of $2,000 for the tax year; and
- taxes deducted will increase for each pay, which will be based on $54,000 instead of $52,000 estimated annual income.

The employee will be paying higher taxes for each pay compared with the 26 pay frequency calculation.

At the beginning of each year, a payroll administrator will determine which pay frequency should be used.

PART 2

Employment Standard Acts

The Ministry of Labour administers the provincial employment standards with regard to minimum wage, public holidays, hours of work, vacation entitlement, leave of absence, termination, severance and more. The Ministry ensures that employer responsibilities and employee rights are in accordance with the Employment Standards Act.

The payroll administrator must understand that the company benefits program and policies are in accordance with the rules and regulations of the Employment Standards Act in order to protect employee rights.

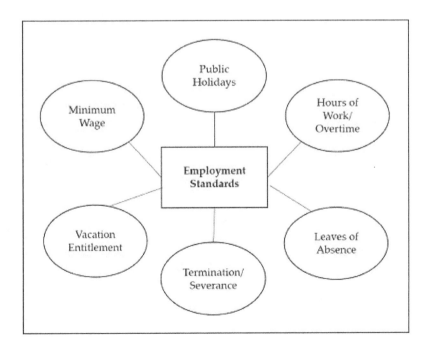

Chapter 4

Employment Standards

4.1 Federal

The chart below is the holiday schedule.

Holiday	2019	2020
New Year's Day	Tue, Jan 1	Wed, Jan 1
Good Friday	Fri, Apr 19	Fri, Apr 10
Easter Monday *	Mon, Apr 22	Mon, Apr 13
Victoria Day	Mon, May 20	Mon, May 18
Canada Day	Mon, July 1	Wed, July 1
Labour Day	Mon, Sep 2	Mon, Sep 7
Thanksgiving Day	Mon, Oct 14	Mon, Oct 12
Remembrance Day	Mon, Nov 11	Wed, Nov 11
Christmas Day	Wed, Dec 25	Fri, Dec 25
Boxing Day	Thu, Dec 26	Sat, Dec 26

* Federal employees only.

- Any statutory holiday that falls on Saturday or Sunday is observed on the following Monday;
- Labour Day is observed on the first Monday in September; and
- Thanksgiving Day is observed on the second Monday in October.

The chart below shows relevant information on Employment Standards for various topics.

Topics	Comments
Minimum Wage	Determined by the rate of the province in which work is performed
Overtime	1-1/2 times pay for each of work over eight hours a day or 40 hours per week
Vacation Entitlement	two weeks of vacation time for up to five years of employment; three weeks of vacation after six years
Vacation Pay	Vacation pay for hourly paid employees are calculated at 4% of vacationable earnings up to five years of service and 6% after six years
Maternity	17 weeks
Parental	37 weeks
Termination Notice	Less than three weeks—nil More than three weeks—two weeks' notice or 2 weeks of pay

4.2   Ontario

4.2.1   Statutory Holidays/Holiday Pay

General holidays are referred to as statutory or "stat" holidays. They are federally and provincially legislated holidays. Employees in Ontario receive a day off, a day off with pay or compensation in lieu of time off.

Holiday	2019	2020
New Year's Day	Tue, Jan 1	Wed, Jan 1
Family Day	Mon, Feb 18	Mon, Feb 17
Good Friday	Fri, Apr 19	Fri, Apr 10
Victoria Day	Mon, May 20	Mon, May 18
Canada Day	Mon, July 1	Wed, July 1
Civic Day *	Mon, Aug 5	Mon, Aug 3
Labour Day	Mon, Sep 2	Mon, Sep 7
Thanksgiving Day	Mon, Oct 14	Mon, Oct 12
Christmas Day	Wed, Dec 25	Fri, Dec 25
Boxing Day	Thu, Dec 26	Sat, Dec 26

* Not a statutory holiday. Employers may choose to offer holiday pay.

- Any statutory holiday that falls on Saturday or Sunday is observed on the following Monday;
- Labour Day is observed on the first Monday in September;
- Thanksgiving Day is observed on the second Monday in October
- Remembrance Day is not a statutory holiday in Ontario; and
- Easter Sunday is not a public holiday, but under the Retail Business Holidays Act businesses are required to be closed.

Last and First Rule

An employee is eligible for holiday pay if the employee worked on the last regular scheduled day of work before the public holiday and the first regular scheduled day after the public holiday.

Holiday Pay

The amount of statutory holiday pay an employee is entitled to is regular wages and the vacation pay in the four weeks before the week of the public holiday divided by 20.

Premium Pay

An employee must be paid 1.5 times their regular rate of pay for each hour worked on a public holiday. For example, if the employee's regular rate of pay is $16 an hour, the premium pay is $24 an hour ($16.00 X 1.5).

Overtime Pay

An employee receives overtime pay of at least 1-1/2 times regular pay after 44 hours of work in a week. Any hours worked on a public holiday are not included in the calculation of overtime hours.

Substitute Holiday

A substitute holiday is another working day off work to replace a public holiday. For the substitute holiday, the employee will be paid the same as the public holiday pay.

4.2.2   Minimum Hourly Rates

Rates below are for hourly-paid employees.

- $14.00 – general worker;
- $12.20 – liquor server;
- $13.15 – students under 16 (less than 28 hours per week);
- $15.40 – homeworkers;
- commission – hourly rate must be at least the minimum wage; and
- the minimum wage rule also applies to salaried employees. For example, if an employee works eight hours a day, 5 five days a week, 52 weeks a year at the minimum wage of $14.00, the annual salary must be at least $29,120 to conform to the Employment Standards Act.

4.2.3   Hours of Work

The maximum daily and weekly limits on hours of work are eight hours a day and 48 hours a week, and employees must be paid for a minimum of three hours if called into work, even if the work is less than three hours. This rule does not apply to an employee whose regular shift is three hours or less.

4.2.4   Overtime Pay

- an employee receives overtime pay of at least 1-1/2 times of regular pay after 44 hours of work in a week;
- it is common practice for some employers to pay overtime for hours worked over eight hours in a day; and
- managers and supervisors do not qualify for overtime pay.

4.2.5   Rest/Eating Periods

The employer must give employees:

- a rest period of 11 consecutive hours in a 24-hour period;
- between shifts, eight hours of rest period;
- in a work week, a rest period of 24 consecutive hours; and
- a 30-minute eating break after five hours of work, which can instead be split into two 15-minute breaks.

4.2.6   Vacation Entitlement/Pay

As a minimum, an employee is entitled to:

- two weeks of vacation time with less than five years of employment;
- three weeks of vacation time with five or more years of employment; and
- an employer may offer more than the minimum allowed; for example, managers and supervisors are usually offered three or more weeks of vacation at the start of employment.

Vacation pay for hourly-paid employees is calculated at:

- 4% of vacationable earnings for employment less than five years; and
- 6% of vacationable earnings for employment after five years.

4.2.7   Leaves of Absence

An employee is entitled to the following leaves of absence:

- Pregnancy Leave—up to 17 weeks, or longer of unpaid time off work;
- Parental Leave—birth mothers can take up to 61 weeks of unpaid time off work. All other new parents can take up to 63 weeks of unpaid time off work;
- Family Medical—unpaid, job-protected leave of up to 28 weeks in a 52-week period;
- Family Responsibility—up to three days per year after they have worked for at least two consecutive weeks. An employee who missed part of a day to take this leave would be entitled to any wages earned while working; and
- Bereavement—up to two days per year.

C h a p t e r   5

Termination/Record of Employment (ROE)

5.1   Termination and Notice

Termination of employment is an employee's departure from a job and the end of an employer and employee relationship. Termination may be voluntary on the employee's part by quitting, or it may be involuntary, often in the form of dismissal or a layoff. An employee may be terminated for a number of reasons: shortage of work, dismissal, poor performance, misconduct, etc.

When an employee has completed less than three months of service before termination, the employer does not have an obligation to provide notice or termination pay. After three months, the employer must provide a written notice of termination letter, termination pay or both that should equal the length of the termination entitlement.

- Termination Notice:
  - o required after employee has worked continuously for three months;
  - o must be a written notice following the ESA chart below;
  - o can terminate employee when notice has expired; and
  - o termination pay must be paid for the remainder of the termination notice if employee was terminated before the notice has expired.

- Termination Pay:
  - o required after employee has worked continuously for three months;
  - o follow the ESA chart below for amount of termination pay; and
  - o termination pay must be paid either seven days after the employee is terminated or on the employee's next regular pay date, whichever is later.

- Employment Standards Act (ESA):

Period of Employment	Notice Required/ Termination Pay
Less than 1 year	1 week
1 year but less than 3 years	2 weeks
3 years but less than 4 years	3 weeks
4 years but less than 5 years	4 weeks
5 years but less than 6 years	5 weeks
6 years but less than 7 years	6 weeks
7 years but less than 8 years	7 weeks
8 years or more	8 weeks

5.2 Severance Pay

Severance pay is a lump-sum payment that is paid to an employee w h o has been involuntarily terminated. It compensates an employee for losses that occur when a long- term employee loses their job. Severance pay is not the same as termination pay, which is given in place of the required notice of termination of employment.

An employee qualifies for severance pay if their employment is severed and:

- they have worked for the employer for five or more years whether continuous or not and whether active or not; and
- their employer has a payroll in Ontario of at least $2.5 million or severed the employment of 50 or more employees in a six-month period because all or part of the business permanently closed.

To calculate severance pay:

- multiply the number of completed years of employment by the employee's weekly wage;
- for a partially completed year of employment, multiply the number of months of completed employment divided by 12 and multiplied by the weekly wage.

The maximum amount of severance pay required to be paid is 26 weeks.

Example of how to calculate severance pay:

- employee works 40 hours a week at $20.00 = $800.00;
- employee was employed for five years and six months;
- severance for five years equals 5 x $800 equals $4,000;
- severance pay for extra six months equals (6 divided by 12) multiplied by $800 equals $400; and
- total severance for five years and six months equals $4,000 plus $400 equals $4,400.

When to pay severance:

- employee must receive severance pay either seven days after the employee's termination or on what would have been the employee's next regular pay day, whichever is later;

- employer may pay severance in installments with agreement from the employee or approval from the Ministry of Labour; and
- an installment plan cannot last more than three years; if the agreement schedule is not followed, severance pay becomes due immediately.

5.3   Record of Employment (ROE)

The ROE is the form, whether electronic or paper, that employers complete for employees receiving insurable earnings who stop working and experience an interruption of earnings. The ROE is the single most important document in the Employment Insurance (EI) program.

The employer must complete the ROE even if the employee does not intend to apply for EI benefits. On the ROE, the employer enters details about the employee's work history with the organization, including insurable earnings and insurable hours.

There are two ROE formats available: electronic or paper.

An employer is required to issue a ROE each time an employee has an interruption of earnings or stoppage of work.

A ROE must be issued when an employee had or is anticipated to have seven consecutive calendar days with no work and no insurable earnings from the employer. This is often referred to as the "7-Day Rule."

The "7-Day Rule" applies when employees quit their jobs or are laid off, employment is terminated, or an employee's salary falls below 60% of regular weekly earnings because of illness, injury, quarantine, pregnancy, the need to care for a newborn child or to provide care or support to a family member who is critically ill.

The responsibility of issuing a ROE falls to the employer, as it is used to determine:

- the individual's eligibility for Employment Insurance benefits;
- the amount of the benefits; and
- how long the individual can receive the benefits.

The ROE must be filed online or given to the employee within five days of the interruption of earnings.

There are two ways to prepare a ROE online and on paper. Each method requires a different lead time, so it is good to plan ahead. If you order the forms by phone from Service Canada, they will be mailed to you within four to ten business days, depending on your location.

However, if you prefer to use the ROE Web program, a designated representative from your company must register in person at a Service Canada Centre before receiving an activation code to be used online. This process could take up to 20 days but only needs to be done once.

Who can prepare a ROE?

- the person responsible for payroll preparation within the company;
- the bookkeeper;
- the accountant; and
- outside payroll preparation service hired by your company.

> An employer does not need to issue a paper copy of the ROE when it is submitted electronically.

5.4   Eligibility to Employment Insurance (EI)

EI benefits are provided to employees if:

- the employee has enough insurable hours;
- the loss of their job was through no fault of their own; and
- they are actively looking for another job.

An employee should always apply for EI benefits after termination as soon as possible. One can apply for benefits even if the Record of Employment (ROE) has not been received.

5.5   Qualifying Period for EI

The qualifying period is the shorter of:

- the 52-week period immediately before the start date of your claim; or
- the period from the start of a previous benefit period to the start of your new benefit period if you applied for benefits earlier and your application was approved in the last 52 weeks.

PART 3

Employee Set Up

One of the more complex payroll issues is determining whether an individual is an employee or a self-employed worker. Although the differences between the two can sometimes appear insignificant, incorrectly assessing the relationship can result in costly repercussions for the employer and the individual.

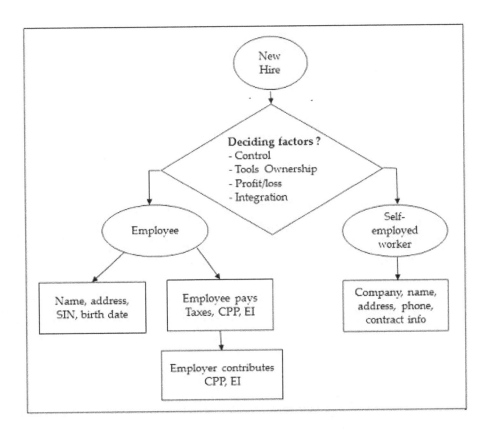

Chapter 6

Employee or Self-Employed Worker

6.1   Establish Employer-Employee Relationship

The hiring process is an essential part of running a business. The recruitment of workers is not necessarily part of payroll; however, the payroll administrator must understand the mechanism of filling a position in the company and responsibilities involved in the procedure.

It is important to decide if the new hire is an employee or a self-employed individual. Employment status directly affects a worker's entitlement to EI benefits under the Employment Insurance Act as well as other legislation such as CPP and the Income Tax Act.

There are key factors to consider in determining employment status by applying the 4-point test, namely:

- control;
- ownership of tools;
- chance of profit/risk of loss; and
- integration.

Using these four points, the CRA checks the relationship between the worker and the employer by considering 2 factors:

- did the worker enter into a contract of service (employer-employee relationship)? or
- did the worker enter into a contract for service as self-employed?

The following chart is a benchmark used by the CRA when assessing whether the individual is an employee or self- employed worker.

Factor	Worker is an Employee	Self-Employed Worker
Control	• subordination to employer • control by employer of how work is performed • employer can assign any work • can receive training and direction for any work	• works without supervision as long as contract is completed • uses own tools and equipment • can accept or refuse to perform work • relationship can be discontinued upon completion of work without recrimination
Tools and Equipment	• employer supplies tools and equipment to perform work assigned • reimbursement of cost for any tools and equipment purchased by employee	• uses own tools and equipment • retains owner-ship and is responsible for the cost of repairs, main-tenance and insurance

Factor	Worker is an Employee	Self-Employed Worker
Financial Risk	• is not responsible for any operating expenses • is not responsible if contract is not completed • has no investment in business • cannot realize profit or loss	• is financially liable if contract is not fulfilled or completed • will not receive any protection or insurance from employer • has made investment, manages staff, can hire and pay others to perform contract with employer
Integration	• work forms an integral part of the business • income comes from work performed for employer	• services rendered are not activities usually performed by employer, therefore contracted • engages in one or more contract

Chapter 7

Employee Payroll Set Up

7.1   Social Insurance Number (SIN)

A Social Insurance Number (SIN) is a nine-digit number used for benefits and services from government programs, income tax, CPP and EI. Every person working in Canada must have a SIN, and each is issued to one person only and not transferrable, and its use is mandatory for payroll processing. Employers must ensure that:

- within three days of starting employment the employee provides a Social Insurance Number. If the first digit of the SIN is a "9" (non-Canadian citizen), the employee must provide proof of date of expiration;
- the SIN is kept confidential and must only be used for payroll purposes; and
- all documents used to validate SIN are copied and filed.

7.2   Payroll Information Required

The following employee information is required for payroll:

- name;
- address;
- date of birth;
- Social Insurance Number;
- bank account number (if applicable)
- Federal TD1 form; and
- Ontario TD1 form.

7.3   Federal and Ontario TD1 Forms

TD1—Personal Tax Credits—is a form used to determine the amount of tax to be deducted from an individual's employment income before taxes are calculated.

An employee must complete or revise a federal and Ontario TD1 Personal Tax Credits form if:

- they are a new hire; or
- they experience life changes that affect the tax credit, such as age, pension income, disability amount, caregiver or eligible dependent.

> If an employee has more than one employer, the personal tax credits can be claimed only once. In this case, the federal and Ontario TD1 forms for the second employer must have "0" entered on lines 2 to 12 in order that the Total Claim Amount on line 13 is zero, which is the amount of the employee's tax credits.

PART 4

Payroll Processing

This section covers preparation and gathering of information required to process a payroll. It explains how taxes, CPP and EI are calculated. It also describes the reporting requirement of a pay statement.

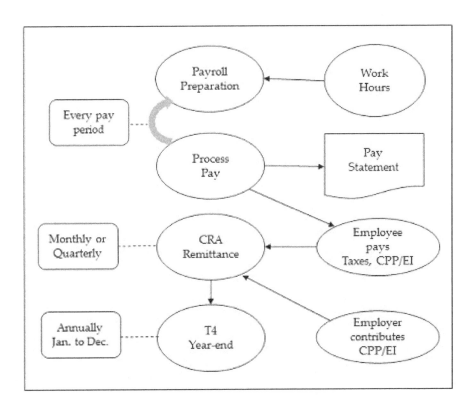

Chapter 8

Calculate Payroll

This section explains how federal and Ontario taxes, CPP contributions and EI premiums are calculated.

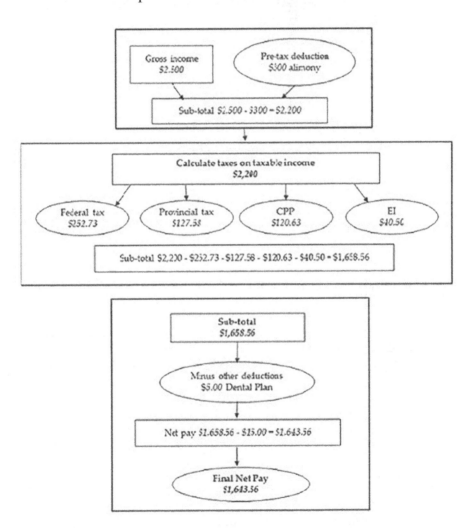

8.1   Federal Taxes

The federal tax is calculated separately from the Ontario tax but combined when reporting in the CRA remittance report. For 2019, refer to Appendix A—2019 Federal Claim Codes. The formula for calculating employee annual federal tax is:

- Code definitions:
  - o   T3 – annual federal tax
  - o   R – federal tax rate
  - o   A – annual taxable income
  - o   K – constant amount
  - o   K1 – non-refundable personal tax credit
  - o   K2 – CPP and EI tax credit
  - o   K3 – other federal tax credits
  - o   K4 – Canada employment amount

- Annual federal tax:
  - o   T3 = (R multiplied by A) minus (K + K1 + K2 + K3 + K4)
  - o   If the result is negative, then the annual federal tax is zero.

The table below lists the 2019 federal tax rates and income thresholds.

Annual taxable income (A) More than – not more than ($)	Rate (R)	Constant ($) (K)
0 - 47,630	0.150	0
47,630 - 95,259	0.205	2,620
95,259 - 47,667	0.260	7,859
147,667 - 10,371	0.290	12,289
210,371 and over	0.330	20,704

- K1 = 0.15 multiplied by the claim amount reported on the federal TD1 form
- K2 = [0.15 multiplied by (# of pay periods multiplied by CPP contributions for the pay period, up to a maximum of $2,748.90)]
- + K2 = [0.15 multiplied by (# of pay periods multiplied by EI premium for the pay period, up to a maximum of $860.22)]
- K3 = other federal credits. If it is the first pay period of the year, then the K3 amount must be adjusted using the formula (# of pay periods multiplied by K3) divided by # of pay periods left in the year
- K4 = the lesser of:
  o 0.15 times the annual taxable income
  o 0.15 times $1,222
- The federal tax (T3) for a pay period equals the annual tax divided by the number of pay periods.

8.2 Ontario Taxes

The Ontario tax is calculated separately from the federal tax but combined when reporting in the CRA remittance report. For 2019, refer to Appendix B—2019 Ontario Claim Codes. The formula for calculating employee annual Ontario tax is:

- code definitions
  o T2 – annual provincial tax deduction
  o T4 – annual provincial tax
  o V – provincial tax rate
  o V1 – provincial surtax
  o V2 – Ontario health premium
  o A – annual taxable income
  o KP – provincial constant
  o K1P – provincial non-refundable personal tax credit

- o K2P – provincial CPP and EI tax credit
- o K3P – other provincial tax credits
- o S – provincial tax reduction
- o LCP – labour sponsored funds tax credit

- T2 = T4 + V1 + V2 – S – LCP
  If the result is negative, T2 = $0
  - o Where:
    T4 = (V x A) – KP – K1P – K2P – K3P
    Where V and KP are based on the value of A in the 2019
    Ontario tax rates and income thresholds table.

The table below is the 2019 Ontario tax rates and income thresholds.

Annual taxable income (A) More than – not more than ($)	Rate (V)	Constant ($) (KP)
0 - 43,906	0.0505	0
43,906 - 87,813	0.0915	1,800
87,813 - 150,000	0.1116	3,565
150,000 - 220,000	0.1216	5,065
220,000 and over	0.1316	7,265

- K1P = 0.0505 × TCP
- K2P = [(0.0505 × (P × C, maximum $2,748.90)) + (0.0505 × (P × EI, maximum $860.22))]
- V1 = Where T4 ≤$4,740
  - o V1 = $0
  - o Where T4 > $4,740 ≤$6,067
  - o V1 = 0.20 × (T4 – $4,740)
  - o Where T4 > $6,067
  - o V1 = 0.20 × (T4 – $4,740) + 0.36 × (T4 – $6,067)

- V2 = Where A ≤$20,000, V2 = $0
  Where A > $20,000 ≤$36,000, V2 = the lesser of:
  (i) $300; and
  (ii) 0.06 × (A – $20,000)

  Where A > $36,000 ≤$48,000, V2 = the lesser of:
  (i) $450; and
  (ii) $300 + (0.06 × (A – $36,000))

  Where A > $48,000 ≤$72,000, V2 = the lesser of:
  (i) $600; and
  (ii) $450 + (0.25 × (A – $48,000))

  Where A > $72,000 ≤$200,000, V2 = the lesser of:
  (i) $750; and
  (ii) $600 + (0.25 × (A – $72,000))

  Where A > $200,000, V2 = the lesser of:
  (i) $900; and
  (ii) $750 + (0.25 × (A – $200,000))
- **S** = The lesser of:
  (i) T4 + V1; and
  (ii) [2 × ($244 + Y)] – [T4 + V1]
- LCP = $0
- The Ontario tax (T2) for a pay period equals the annual tax divided by the number of pay periods.

8.3 Canada Pension Plan (CPP)

For 2019, the following are the rates for CPP:

- maximum pensionable earnings are $57,400;
- annual basic exemption is $3,500;
- employee contribution rate is 5.1%; and
- maximum employee annual contribution is $2,748.90.

The formula for calculating employee CPP contribution per pay period is:

- CPP contribution is the lesser of:
  o $2,748.90 minus the employee CPP contribution year to date;
  o basic exemption equals $3,500 divided by the number of pay periods; and
  o CPP contribution is 5.1% multiplied by gross wages minus the basic exemption.

Example A shows how a regular CPP contribution is calculated. Example B shows how CPP contribution calculation is done when the CPP annual maximum is reached.

- Example A: if the bi-weekly gross wage is $5,000, year- to-date CPP contribution is $1,000:
  o Calculation 1: $2,748.90 minus $1,000 equals $1,748.90;
  o basic exemption is $3,500, divided by 26 pay period equals $134.62;
  o Calculation 2: $5,000 minus $134.62 multiplied by 5.1% equals $248.13; and
  o CPP contribution is the lesser of Calculation 1 and Calculation 2 equals $248.13.

- Example B: if the bi-weekly gross wage is $5,000, year-to-date CPP contribution is $2,600:
  o Calculation 1: $2,748.90 minus $2,600 equals $148.90;
  o basic exemption is $3,500, divided by 26 pay period equals $134.62;
  o Calculation 2: $5,000 minus $134.62 multiplied by 5.1% equals $248.13; and
  o CPP contribution is the lesser of Calculation 1 and Calculation 2 equals $148.90.

8.4   Employment Insurance (EI)

For 2019, the following are the rates for EI:

- maximum insurable earnings are $53,100;
- premium rate is 1.62%; and
- employee maximum premium is $860.22.

The formula for calculating employee EI premium per pay period is the lesser of:

- $860.22 minus the employee year-to-date EI premium; and
- 1.62% multiplied by insurance earnings.

Example A shows how a regular EI premium is calculated.
Example B shows how an EI premium calculation is done when the EI annual maximum is reached.

- Example A: if the bi-weekly gross wage is $5,000, year- to-date EI premium is $500:
  - o Calculation 1: $860.22 minus $500 equals $360.22;
  - o Calculation 2: 1.62% multiplied by $5,000 equals $81; and
  - o EI premium is the lesser of Calculation 1 and Calculation 2 equals $81.

- Example B: if the bi-weekly gross wage is $5,000, year- to-date EI premium is $800:
  - o Calculation 1: $860.22 minus $800 equals $60.22;
  - o Calculation 2: 1.62% multiplied by $5,000 equals $81; and
  - o EI premium is the lesser of Calculation 1 and Calculation 2 equals $60.22.

Chapter 9

Pay Statement

9.1 Pay Statement

An accurate pay statement, commonly called a pay stub, is required under the Employment Standards Act for all provinces, as shown in the example below.

Pay Period 1 (January 2019)

Province of employment: Ontario
Number of pay periods: 26 - Bi-weekly

ABC Company
123 Buckingham Street

		Federal TD1 (Code 1):	$12,069.00
		Provincial TD1 (Code 1):	$10,582.00
		Pay Date:	Jan 04, 2019

Name: **John Smith**

	Hours/ %	Income	Deductions	Total
Gross pay	96.00h @$14.0000	$1,344.00		
Holiday pay (1.5)	8.00h @$14.0000 * 1.50	$168.00		
Overtime pay (1.5)	6.00h @$14.0000 * 1.50	$126.00		
Vacation pay (by %)	$1,638.00 @ 4.00%	$65.52		
Total Gross Income				**$1,703.52**
Medical & Dental Benefits(EmployeR)		$20.00		
Total Non-Cash Income		$20.00		
Federal Tax			$165.55	
ON Provincial Tax			$79.74	
Employment Insurance			$27.60	
CPP			$81.03	
Total Taxes, EI, CPP				**($353.92)**
Medical & Dental Benefits(EmployeE)			$20.00	
Total Deductions				**($20.00)**
			Net Pay	**$1,329.60**

The employer must establish a recurring pay period and pay all wages earned in that period.

The following is required on a pay statement:

- pay period for which the wages are being paid;
- employee's hourly rate (if one exists);
- gross amount of wages—before taxes and other deductions—and how it was calculated;
- amount and description of each earnings and deductions;
- taxes, CPP contribution and EI premium; and
- net pay.

There is other information that could be included in a pay statement, including:

- company name and address;
- employee name;
- province of employment and pay frequency;
- pay date;
- federal and Ontario tax claim codes;
- breakdown of gross pay, including regular wages, overtime and vacation pay;
- how vacation and overtime (if any) were calculated;
- breakdown of statutory (mandatory) government deductions; and
- other deductions such as benefit co-pays, parking fees, etc.

PART 5

T4 Processing and CRA Remittance

This section describes payroll year-end processing, which consists of issuing T4 slips to employees and submitting copies of T4 slips and a summary to CRA using paper or electronic filings.

Employer Health Tax (EHT) and Workplace Safety & Insurance Board (WSIB) reports and payments have to be filed at year-end to each respective government agency.

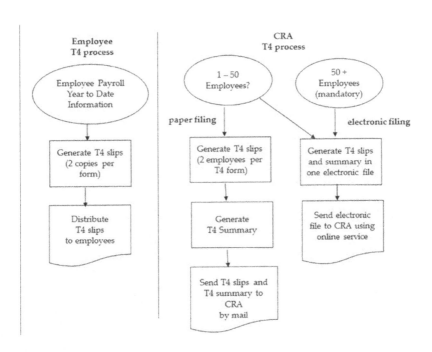

Chapter 10

CRA Remittance

10.1   CRA Remittance

Sample form needed CRA PD7A Form Remittance Form.

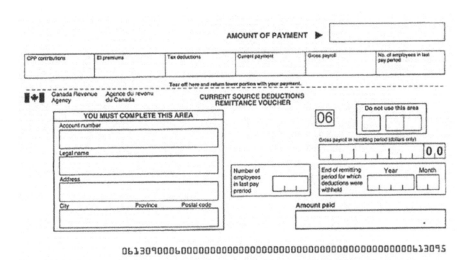

The fields required for remitting the CRA monthly or quarterly form are:

- pay period covered;
- tax deduction for employee;
- CPP contributions of both employer and employee;
- EI premiums of both employer and employee;
- current payment—total of taxes, CPP and EI;
- gross payroll—total gross pay for the periods covered; and
- number of employees in period covered.

Ch a p t e r 11

Year - end Processing

11.1   Employer Responsibilities

The employer is responsible for the following:

- Employee T4 slip
  - o prepare and distribute two copies of T4 slips to employees on or before the last day of February; and
  - o Box 54 (Employer's payroll account number) must be blank.

- CRA filing on paper
  - o only allowed for 50 or less employees, otherwise there will be penalties imposed by the CRA;
  - o complete a T4 Summary form;
  - o send duplicate copies of all T4s and T4 summary to CRA on or before the last day of February; and
  - o T4 copies to CRA should contain two employees in a single sheet of paper.

- CRA electronic filing
  - o mandatory electronic filing for more than 50 employees, however, electronic filing can be done for any number of employees; and
  - o generate an XML-language based electronic file (produced by using a payroll software) and send online to CRA. This electronic file must contain the summary information and filed on or before the last day of February.

- Records must be kept for six years. Early destruction of records requires permission from the CRA by submitting a Form T137, *Request for Destruction of Records.*

11.2   T4 Slip

Sample form of a T4 slip.

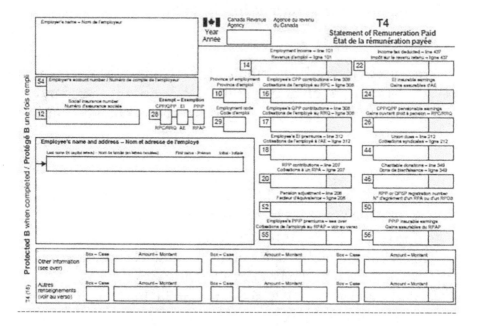

Tips for completing the T4 slip:

- enter all amounts in Canadian dollars;
- do not use the $ sign, any other special characters or negative amounts; and
- if an employee works in different provinces, separate T4 slips have to be filed in each province.

The following are the fields on the T4 form:

- tax year
- box 10 – province of employment
- box 12 – social insurance number
- box 14 – employment income
- box 16 – employee's CPP contributions
- box 18 – employee's EI premiums
- box 22 – income tax deducted
- box 24 – EI insurable earnings
- box 26 – CPP pensionable earnings
- box 28 – CPP or EI exempt
- box 29 – employment code
- box 44 – union dues
- box 46 – charitable donations
- box 50 – RPP or DPSP registration number
- box 52 – pension adjustment
- box 54 – employer's account number
- codes 30 to 88, other information, e.g. code 40—taxable benefits

> Box 54 of the T4 slip is the employer's business account number. This field for the employee's copy must be blank, but must be filled in for the CRA copy.

11.3   T4 Summary

Sample form of a T4 summary.

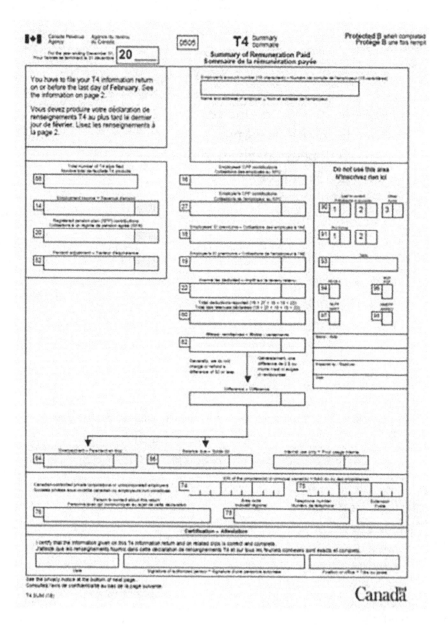

If you are filing your return electronically, do not send the paper copy of the slips or summary.

Tips for completing the T4 summary:

- enter all amounts in Canadian dollars;
- do not use the $ sign, any other special characters or negative amounts; and
- file a separate T4 summary for each payroll account.

The following are the fields on the T4 form:

- tax year
- line 14 – employment income
- line 16 – employee's CPP contributions
- line 18 – employee's EI premiums
- line 19 – employer's EI premiums
- line 20 – Registered Pension Plan (RPP) contributions
- line 22 – income tax deducted
- line 27 – employer's CPP contribution
- line 52 – pension adjustment
- lines 74 and 75 – Canadian controlled private corporations or unincorporated employers
- lines 76 and 88 – person to contact
- line 80 – total deductions reported
- line 82 – minus: remittances – enter the amount you remitted for the year
- difference – subtract line 82 from line 80
- line 84 – overpayment
- line 86 – balance due
- line 88 – total number of T4 slips filed

11.4 Penalty for T4 Late Filing

An employer must give an employee their T4 slips and file T4 information to the CRA on or before the last day of February for the taxation year. If the last day of February falls on a weekend, submission deadline is the next business day.

The table below illustrates penalties that will applied for late submission.

Number of Information Returns (slips filed late)	Penalty per day (up to 100 days)	Maximum Penalty
1 to 5	Penalty not based on number of days	$100 flat penalty
6 to 10	$5	$500
11 to 50	$10	$1,000
51 to 500	$15	$1,500
501 to 2,500	$25	$2,500
2,501 to 10,000	$60	$5,000
10,001 or more	$75	$7,500

11.5 Mandatory Electronic Filing Penalty

Paper filing is only limited to 50 T4 slips. Any additional T4 slips submitted will incur the following penalties as shown on the table below:

Number of information Returns (slips) by type	Penalty
51 to 250	$250
251 to 500	$500
501 to 2,500	1,500
2,501 or more	$2,500

11.6   EHT Reporting

For 2019, the EHT exemption amount is $490,000. An employer has to pay EHT if the annual payroll exceeds the EHT exemption. If the payroll exceeds $5 million, the employer is not eligible for the EHT exemption. However, eligible employers who are registered charities can claim the exemption even if their payroll exceeds $5 million.

EHT rates vary from 0.98% on Ontario payroll less than $200,000, and up to 1.95% for payroll in excess of $400,000.

The amount of EHT an employer pays is calculated by multiplying Ontario payroll for the year, after deducting any tax exemption, by the applicable tax rate. The tax rate is based on the Ontario payroll of the employer before deducting any tax exemption.

2019 EHT Tax Rate

Ontario Payroll (Total Remuneration)	Rate (%)
Up to $200,000.00	0.98%
$200,000.01 to $230,000.00	1.101%
$230,000.01 to $260,000.00	1.223%
$260,000.01 to $320,000.00	1.344%
$290,000.01 to $320,000.00	1,465%
$320,000.01 to $350,000.00	1.586%
$350,000.01 to $380,000.00	1.708%
$380,000.01 to $400,000.00	1.829%
Over $400,000.00	1.95%

For example, an employer with $175,000 of payroll who does not have any tax exemption, would have a tax rate of 0.98%, and would pay EHT of $1,715 for the year.

Instalment payments are applicable if:

- employers with an annual payroll over $600,000 have to make monthly EHT instalment payments;
- employers who are eligible for a tax exemption and who have payroll over $600,000 have to make monthly instalments as soon as their payroll exceeds their allowable exemption amount; and
- employers with an annual payroll of $600,000 or less do not need to make instalment payments.

Due dates for filing EHT returns:

- annual returns are due March 15th of the following calendar year;
- special returns are due on the 15th of the month after the payroll was paid; and
- final returns are due 40 days after a company closure or the amalgamation date.

> Financial institutions are not authorized to accept or process EHT returns

PART 6

Using a Free Online Tool to do Payroll

Using the case scenario below, the WinTax Free Calculator (www.hrclub.ca) gives examples of how taxes, CPP and EI are calculated. Information is also provided to show how CRA remittance amounts are calculated.

Chapter 12

Case Scenario

Employee Name	John Smith
Company Name	ABC Company
Province	Ontario
Pay Frequency	Bi-Weekly
Hourly Rate	$14.00
Hours Worked	96
Holiday Pay	8 hours
Overtime	6 hours
Vacation	4%
Medical & Dental Benefits (Employer)	$20
Medical & Dental Benefits (Employee)	$20

Chapter 13

WinTax Free Calculator Example

13.1 Generating Pay Statement

The following steps will show you how to the process a payroll by:

- calculating employee taxes, CPP and EI;
- processing CRA remittance; and
- processing T4 for year-end.

Below is the Data Entry Screen of the WinTax free calculator.

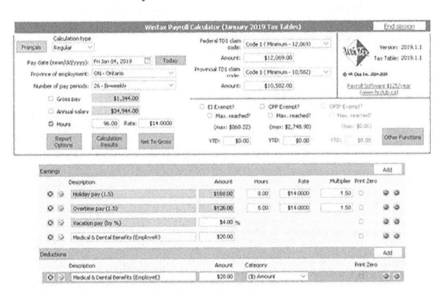

STEP 1 **Calculation Type**: Choose the drop-down menu and select 'Regular.'

STEP 2 **Pay Date**: Choose the pay date your employee is paid using the calendar icon—for example, 'Fri Jan 04, 2019.'

STEP 3 **Province of Employment**: In this scenario, we will be using the Province of Ontario.

STEP 4 **Number of Pay Periods**: Using the drop down box, select '26 – Biweekly.'

STEP 5 **Hours:** Select the 'Hourly' field to enter the work hours and hourly rate. In this case, the employee worked 96 hours in a bi-weekly payroll (assuming first week 46 hours and the second week 50 hours). Overtime in Ontario is calculated after an employee has worked 44 hours in a work week. Calculate the employee's overtime hours before entering the regular hours.

- Overtime 1st week (46 minus 44) = 2 hours overtime
- Overtime 2nd week (50 minus 44) = 6 hours overtime
- Total overtime = 8 hours
- **Total Regular Hours: (96 minus 8) = 88 regular hours**

STEP 6 **Rate**: Enter '$14.00' in the rate field.

STEP 7 **Federal & Provincial TD1 Claim**: By default, code 1 will give the minimum basic exemption. If an employee fills out the TD1 form and claims tax credits, then you must choose the proper code for both federal and provincial taxes.

STEP 8   **EI & CPP Exemptions:** For this example, wages paid to business owners and shareholders with more than 40% ownership are not subject to EI benefits.

Employees under the age of 18 and over age 70 do not contribute to CPP.

EMPLOYEE EARNINGS

STEP 9   **Holiday Pay (1.5):** Enter the total number of hours calculated in Step 5 (8 hours), then enter the rate and the system will automatically calculate the holiday pay amount at 1.5 times the hourly rate.

STEP 10   **Overtime Pay (1.5):** Enter the total number of hours calculated in Step 5 (6 hours), then enter the rate and the system will automatically calculate the overtime amount at 1.5 times the hourly rate.

STEP 11   **Vacation pay (by %):** Generally, an employee is entitled to two weeks' vacation per year, which is equivalent to paying 4% of wages earned for every pay.

STEP 12   **Medical & Dental (Employer):** Enter $20.00. Benefits paid by the employer, for example, medical and dental, are considered non-cash taxable benefits. Non-cash taxable benefits are not insurable for EI.

EMPLOYEE DEDUCTION

STEP 13   **Medical & Dental (Employee):** Enter $20.00. Benefits paid by the employee, for example, medical and dental, are a deduction.

CALCULATING PAY

STEP 14 **Calculation Results**: Click the 'Calculation Results' button to show the pay statement, which is a breakdown of earnings, benefits, deductions and the employee's net pay.

Pay Period 1 (January 2019)

Province of employment: Ontario
Number of pay periods: 26 - Bi-weekly

ABC Company
123 Buckingham Street

		Federal TD1 (Code 1):		$12,069.00
		Provincial TD1 (Code 1):		$10,582.00
		Pay Date:		Jan 04, 2019

Name: **John Smith**

	Hours/ %	Income	Deductions	Total
Gross pay	96.00h @$14.0000	$1,344.00		
Holiday pay (1.5)	8.00h @$14.0000 * 1.50	$168.00		
Overtime pay (1.5)	6.00h @$14.0000 * 1.50	$126.00		
Vacation pay (by %)	$1,638.00 @ 4.00%	$65.52		
Total Gross Income				**$1,703.52**
Medical & Dental Benefits(EmployeR)		$20.00		
Total Non-Cash Income		$20.00		
Federal Tax			$165.55	
ON Provincial Tax			$79.74	
Employment Insurance			$27.60	
CPP			$81.03	
Total Taxes, EI, CPP				**($353.92)**
Medical & Dental Benefits(EmployeE)			$20.00	
Total Deductions				**($20.00)**
			Net Pay	**$1,329.60**

Once you have reviewed your calculation, you can print the pay statement to give to your employees.

STEP 15 **Report Options:** This button will allow you to show the following:

1. Employee name
2. Employer name and address
3. Report title
4. Additional information
   - o gross income
   - o federal and provincial taxable income
   - o taxable benefits
   - o EI insurable earnings
   - o pensionable earnings

5. CRA remittance
   o CPP contribution (employee and employer)
   o EI premiums (employee and employer)
   o tax deduction (employee)

For CPP contribution, employer contribution matches the employee's. For EI contribution, employer contribution is 1.4 times the employee's.

13.2 CRA Remittance and Payroll Year-end Processing

Below is the screen that shows the information required for CRA remittance.

Pay Period 1 (January 2019)

Province of employment: Ontario
Number of pay periods: 26 - Bi-weekly

ABC Company
123 Buckingham Street

		Federal TD1 (Code 1):	$12,069.00
		Provincial TD1 (Code 1):	$10,582.00
		Pay Date:	Jan 04, 2019

Name: **John Smith**

	Hours/ %	Income	Deductions	Total
Gross pay	96.00h @$14.0000	$1,344.00		
Holiday pay (1.5)	8.00h @$14.0000 * 1.50	$168.00		
Overtime pay (1.5)	6.00h @$14.0000 * 1.50	$126.00		
Vacation pay (by %)	$1,638.00 @ 4.00%	$65.52		
Total Gross Income				**$1,703.52**
Medical & Dental Benefits(EmployeR)			$20.00	
Total Non-Cash Income			$20.00	
Federal Tax			$165.55	
ON Provincial Tax			$79.74	
Employment Insurance			$27.60	
CPP			$81.03	
Total Taxes, EI, CPP				**($353.92)**
Medical & Dental Benefits(EmployeE)			$20.00	
Total Deductions				**($20.00)**
			Net Pay	**$1,329.60**

Additional Information	Amount
Gross income	$1,723.52
Taxable income (Federal)	$1,723.52
Taxable income (ON)	$1,723.52
Taxable benefits	$20.00
EI insurable earnings	$1,703.52
Pensionable earnings	$1,723.52

CRA Remittance:	Employee	Rate	Employer	Total
CPP contribution	$81.03	1.000	$81.03	$162.06
EI premiums	$27.60	1.400	$38.64	$66.24
Tax deductions	$245.29			$245.29
Current Payment				**$473.59**

The payroll administrator should keep a running total of every employee's year-to-date earnings and deductions, which can be performed manually in an Excel spreadsheet. This manual method for processing payroll, however, is tedious and error prone and the use of payroll software is highly recommended.

For processing CRA remittance, refer to Chapter 13, and for T4 year-end, refer to Chapter 14.

PART 7

TopTenPayrollConcepts

Chapter 14

Payroll Concepts You Should Know

14.1   CRA Tax Year

The CRA taxation year is from January to December, which is based on the *actual pay dates*. The "year" of the pay dates determines which CRA tax year is filed.

For example, wages earned for work performed in December 2018 and paid in January 2019 will be reported in the 2019 CRA tax year filing.

14.2   Pay Frequency

Once every several years, a weekly payroll will have 53 pays instead of the regular 52. A bi-weekly payroll will have 27 pays instead of 26. This is due to the fact that there are 365 days in a year and 366 days every 4 years on a leap year. This situation affects payroll in important ways in the calculation of taxes.

For example, if the pay is $1,000 per week, the projected annual salary for 52 weeks is $52,000 and for 53 weeks, it is $53,000. Therefore, taxes deducted for the year with the wrong pay frequency will be incorrect.

A best practice is to review your processing schedule at the beginning of the year to ensure your system and/or payroll is set up with the correct pay frequency.

14.3   How Basic Taxes Are Calculated

Taxes calculated are the total of federal and provincial payments and are calculated using different tax tables.

The employee's tax bracket is dependent on their estimated annual income. For example, if their gross pay is $5,000 and the pay frequency is monthly, the estimated annual salary is $60,000.

Taxes are calculated based on taxable earnings. CPP contributions are based on pensionable earnings, and EI premiums are based on insurable earnings.

The amounts used to calculate taxes, CPP and EI are based on different types of earnings. Other earnings such as severance pay are not CPP pensionable but taxable. Deductions such as alimony affect taxes but do not affect the CPP and EI calculations. Taxable benefits are not EI insurable but taxable.

14.4   CPP Contribution Calculation

For 2019, the maximum CPP employee annual contribution is $2,748.90. The contribution rate is 5.1% of pensionable earnings.

A common mistake some administrators make when doing manual calculations is forgetting to consider the annual $3,500 exemption amount.

The formula for calculating CPP contribution is as follows:

- the lesser of:
  - $2,748.90 minus the employee's year-to-date CPP contribution;
  - .051 multiplied by [pensionable income minus ($3,500 divided by the number of pay periods)].

    If the result is negative, then contribution is $0.

14.5   CPP Exemption

Employees under the age of 18 and over the age of 70 do not contribute to CPP.

14.6   EI Exemption

Business owners and shareholders with more than 40% ownership are not eligible to be insured with the EI plan and no premium is deducted from their pay.

14.7   Employee Health Premium

The employee health premium is calculated and deducted from wages earned, which is included as part of the Ontario Provincial Tax and is not generally shown as a separate deduction in a pay statement.

The Employee Health Premium calculation is shown in Chapter 8.2.

14.8   Rounding Discrepancies in Calculations

When calculating taxes, CPP contributions and EI premiums, administrators are faced with how to round the third decimal number. For example, to round 5.736 to 2 decimal places, it will either round to 5.73 or 5.74. The third decimal number when dropped becomes 5.73 or when rounded up (third digit is 5 to 9) becomes 5.74.

The CRA is aware of this anomaly and are lenient in dealing with minor number discrepancies.

14.9   Increase/Decrease of Tax Payment

An employee is allowed to pay additional taxes on top of the calculated tax payment per pay.

An employee cannot request for a specific tax amount to be deducted from a pay. Adjusting tax payments can be requested by filing a Federal TD-1 and/or Provincial TD-1 form with the employer.

14.10   In-house Payroll Processing

Adequate time must be allocated when processing payroll in-house to account for unforeseen events, such as power outages or computer/ internet problems. Payroll processing should be completed one or two days before the cheque due date.

There should be a proper backup/recovery plan in place. Payroll data should be backed up to a source like external drives or cloud-based storage.

PART 8

Appendices

For feedback, corrections and suggestions, please email:
feedback@hrclub.ca

Government websites, sample forms, guides and future updates discussed in this book will be available at www.hrclub.ca/book

Appendix A - 2019 Federal Claim Code

Claim Code	Total claim amount $	Option 1, TC = ($)	Option 1, K1 = ($)
0	No claim amount	0.00	0.00
1	12,069.00	12,069.00	1,810.35
2	12,069.01 - 14,375.00	13,222.00	1,810.35
3	14,375.01 - 16,681.00	15,528.00	2,329.20
4	16,681.01 - 18,897.00	17,834.00	2,675.10
5	18,987.01 - 21,293.00	20,140.00	3,021.00
6	21,983.01 - 23,599.00	22,446.00	3,366.90
7	23,599.01 - 25,905.00	24,752.00	3,712.80
8	25,905.01 - 28,211.00	27,058.00	4,058.70
9	28,211.01 - 30,517.00	29,364.00	4,404.60
10	30,517.01 - 32,823.00	31,670.00	4,750.50

Appendix B - 2019 Ontario Claim Code

Claim Code	Total claim amount $	Option 1, TCP= ($)	Option 1, K1P = ($)
0	No claim amount	0.00	0.00
1	10,582.00	10,582.00	534.39
2	10,582.01 - 12,862.00	11,722.00	591.96
3	12,862.01 - 15,142.00	14,022.00	707.10
4	16,205.01 - 17,422.00	16,282.00	822.24
5	17,422.01 - 19,702.00	18,562.00	937.38
6	19,702.01 - 21,982.00	20,842.00	1.052.52
7	21,982.01 - 24,262.00	23,122.00	1,167.66
8	24,262.01 - 26,542.00	25,402.00	1,282.80
9	26,542.01 - 28,822.00	27,682.00	1,397.94
10	28,822.01 - 31,102.00	29,962.00	1,813.08

Appendix C - T4 XML Electronic File - Sample

XML—Extensible Markup Language—is a markup language that defines a set of rules for encoding documents in a format that is both human-readable and machine-readable

Below is a partial example of a T4 XML electronic file:

```xml
<T4Slip>
  <EMPE_NM>
      <snm>Sample</snm>
      <gvn_nm>Employee</gvn_nm>
  </EMPE_NM>
  <EMPE_ADDR>
      <addr_l1_txt>78 Burlington Street</addr_l1_txt>
      <addr_l2_txt>Unit 567</addr_l2_txt>
      <cty_nm>Burlington</cty_nm>
      <prov_cd>ON</prov_cd>
      <cntry_cd>CAN</cntry_cd>
      <pstl_cd>L7Z5T5</pstl_cd>
  </EMPE_ADDR>
  <sin>123456782</sin>
  <empe_nbr>000000001</empe_nbr>
  <bn>123456782RP0001</bn>
  <cpp_qpp_xmpt_cd>0</cpp_qpp_xmpt_cd>
  <ei_xmpt_cd>0</ei_xmpt_cd>
  <rpt_tcd>O</rpt_tcd>
  <empt_prov_cd>ON</empt_prov_cd>
  <T4_AMT>
      <empt_incamt>2000.00</empt_incamt>
      <cpp_cntrb_amt>85.68</cpp_cntrb_amt>
      <empe_eip_amt>33.20</empe_eip_amt>
      <itx_ddct_amt>209.98</itx_ddct_amt>
      <ei_insu_ern_amt>2000.00</ei_insu_ern_amt>
      <cpp_qpp_ern_amt>2000.00</cpp_qpp_ern_amt>
  </T4_AMT>
  <OTH_INFO/>
</T4Slip>
```

Appendix D - **Social Insurance Number Verification**

The nine-digit Social Insurance Number (SIN) uses the 'Luhn Algorithm' method to verify that the last digit of the SIN is a valid number for the eight digits before it.

For example, for the SIN 273987132, '27398713' is the number and the last digit '2' is the check digit number. Only '2' can be the last digit for the SIN 273987132 to be a valid SIN.

The following is an example on how to calculate and check digit x.

SIN	2	7	3	2	4	6	1	3	x
Double every other	4	14	6	4	8	12	2	6	x
Sum the digits.	4	5	6	4	8	3	2	6	x

- sum of the third row is 38;
- subtract the last digit of 38 which is '8' from 10
- the check digit x is 2

The Luhn algorithm will detect any single-digit error, as well as almost all transpositions of adjacent digits. It will not, however, detect transposition of the two-digit sequence 27 to 72 (or vice versa).